# WELCOME TO INCHMAHOME PRIORY

Inchmahome Priory was established in 1238, on the largest of three islands in the Lake of Menteith. Today the island is a site of national importance, both for the priory ruins and for its natural beauty.

The priory was founded by Walter Comyn, Earl of Mentieth, one of the great magnates of his time. The ancient earldom of Menteith had its chief seat on the adjacent island of Inch Talla and the history of the two islands is intimately linked. The priory offered spiritual solace and peace to the resident community of Augustinian canons, their patrons, benefactors, parishioners and visitors until the mid-1500s, when the Protestant Reformation brought monastic life to a close.

The trees and flowers bring colour to the ruins in spring and the quiet presence of the wildlife living on the lake augments the beauty of the island. Today visitors to the island can share the tranquillity enjoyed by its medieval inhabitants.

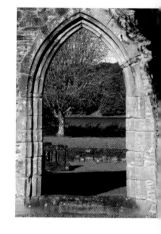

**Above:** The doorway from the choir into the sacristy.

**Opposite:** Inside the chapter house.

## CONTENTS

# INCHMAHOME PRIORY: HIGHLIGHTS

The remains of the Augustinian monastery of Inchmahome are situated on a picturesque island in the Lake of Menteith.

The monastic church and cloister buildings are now largely ruined, although it is still possible to picture how they would have been used. The chapter house in the east range underwent major structural changes when it was converted into a mausoleum in the 17th century. It now houses a fine collection of carved stones.

In 1547, the child Mary Queen of Scots stayed at Inchmahome for three weeks. A bower of boxwood trees remains as a tangible relic of her time here.

The priory was abandoned shortly after the Reformation of 1560. However, its handsome ruins gained new life as a tourist attraction in the 19th century, complemented by the natural beauty of the island.

## A PLACE OF WORSHIP

### THE BELLTOWER
Probably a later addition to the original building, the tower occupies an unusual position at the NW corner of the nave (p.9).

### THE AISLE ARCADE
Another irregular feature, the handsome arches along the north aisle of the priory church are mostly still standing (p.9).

### THE EAST WINDOW
One of the most striking features of the choir at the east end of the priory church is this tall, elegant window, carved with protruding faces (p.10).

## A PLACE OF RESIDENCE

### THE CLOISTER
The domestic buildings were arranged around an enclosed quadrangle or garth, which still forms the centre of the ruined priory (p.12).

### THE CHAPTER HOUSE
The administrative centre of the priory, where the canons held daily meetings; now used to house a fine collection of medieval graveslabs (p.14).

### THE WARMING HOUSE
Only one room in the priory was heated for the benefit of the canons, who lived, prayed and worked here all year round (p.16).

**Above:** The cloister and chapter house viewed from the SW.

## PERSONAL HISTORIES

### THE SINNING NUN
According to legend, a nun was caught in carnal sin with a scion of the Mentieth family and was buried in an upright position on the island (p.18).

### MARY QUEEN OF SCOTS
Mary was brought to the island for her safety in 1547. The four-year-old queen spent three weeks living here (p.30).

### R.B. CUNNINGHAME GRAHAM
A prominent and colourful figure in Scottish politics from the 1880s to the 1930s, Cunninghame Graham is buried in the priory church (p.31).

## NATURAL BEAUTIES

### THE ISLAND
A quick stroll round the island provides a taste of the surroundings enjoyed by the canons and a glimpse of Inch Talla. Don't miss the centuries-old sweet chestnut trees (p.18).

### THE LAKE
Scotland's only lake is a tranquil and attractive spot, still used for fishing and curling (p.18).

### THE WILDLIFE
The area is abundant with a wide variety of wildlife (p.19).

# A SHORT TOUR OF INCHMAHOME PRIORY

A more detailed tour of the site begins on page 6. This brief description provides an overview of the entire complex.

The largest and most important building is the priory church, the building nearest the shore. It is probably on the site of an earlier parish church, used by the canons before their building was completed. Work started on the most sacred part of the church, the east end (**1**), shortly after foundation. The nave (**2**) was probably completed around five years later. The belltower (**3**) is in an unusual position at the NW corner of the nave and was probably added later.

Inch Talla

To the south of the church are domestic buildings arranged around the cloister (**4**). The cloister buildings survive in a fragmentary state, but it is still possible to make out what most of them were used for.

The chapter house (**5**) is on the ground floor of the east range, below the dormitory. It underwent major alterations in the 17th century to become a mausoleum, and now shelters a collection of rare medieval memorials, originally from the priory church. Next to this is the slype or parlour (**6**), the only place in the monastic complex where conversation was allowed. The remains of the warming house and kitchen (**7**) and drains for the reredorter or latrine block (**8**) take up the rest of the ground floor. The dormitory stretched across the whole of the first floor of the east range.

The south and west ranges are preserved only as foundations. The south range (**9**) housed the refectory on its first floor. The foundations to the south and west are the remains of other unidentified buildings.

Little remains of the west range. This may have been accommodation for the prior and the cellarer, a senior canon responsible for provisioning the priory. There were probably other buildings associated with the priory on the island and around the lake which have not survived at all, as the priory was quarried for building stone after the Reformation.

Inchmahome contains a wealth of fine trees, avenues, shrubs and flowers, and visitors are welcome to explore the island and appreciate its natural beauty.

**This page:** The finely carved masonry on the western façade of the priory church.

**Opposite:** A detail of the west entrance.

# THE PRIORY CHURCH

T he priory church was the heart of all activity on the island, where the canons spent most of their day. It remains the most impressive building of the complex.

Our tour begins in front of the fine west door. This was the processional entrance and would have been used by the canons on important occasions. The impressive ceremonial entrance resembles that of Dunblane Cathedral, suggesting that the same masons may have worked on both buildings. Inchmahome Priory was in the diocese of Dunblane and retained close links with the cathedral. Before Mass on Sundays, this doorway would have framed a double line of canons dressed in white as they processed up the nave, chanting and singing amid incense and glowing candles.

Today the bare stones of the church are starkly visible, but this is deceptive. Before the Reformation, this building would have been plastered and painted in bright colours. Scenes from the Bible would have adorned the walls and statues would have stood in niches, picked out in red and gold and there would have been brightly coloured altar cloths. The vaulted ceiling may have been painted blue and flecked with gold stars and the columns decorated with geometric patterns. The whole space was lit by candles and by sunlight, colourfully tinted by stained glass in the arched windows. Set into the worn and uneven stone floor were the graves of past priors and important benefactors.

Crucially, the church would not have been an open space as it is today. Timber and stone screens demarcated individual chapels within the space and divided the choir from the nave. The positions and dedications of the altars in the nave and choir determined the route taken by religious processions through the church and gave the building its own unique identity.

# THE NAVE

The western half of the church, the nave, was the most accessible part of the priory. Lay visitors would have worshipped here, entering the church via a modest door in the north wall, just east of the belltower.

Unlike monks, all canons were priests and had a duty to minister to populations in the vicinity of their house. However, not all Augustinian houses fulfilled this duty to the same degree. Before the mid–15th century the parish church at Port of Menteith had been moved off the island to the mainland, and although the priory supported the parish priest, ordinary parishioners probably did not use the priory church after this date.

The earl and countess of Mentieth, their family and retainers lived on the neighbouring island of Inch Talla and would have worshipped here. On occasion though, the earl and countess and their immediate family may have been permitted to sit with the canons in their choir.

The nave has some curious features. It is noticeably wider at the west end than at the east, so the south wall is not parallel with the arches along the north side. Similarly, the columns which support the arches do not line up with the buttresses that supported the north wall. The belltower is another oddity, which seems to have been slotted into the last bay of the aisle on the north side at a later date.

When the canons originally settled on the island, they may have taken up residence in an existing church and added to the east end to provide accommodation for their services. The older church may have been gradually incorporated into the fabric of the present building. There is no way to be certain of this, but it might explain the ill-fitting architectural features.

**Left:** A view from the nave into the choir and presbytery.

**Above:** The arches that once separated the nave from the north aisle and belltower.

# THE CHOIR

The choir in the eastern half of the church was formally closed off from the nave by a rood screen (so called because it had a giant rood, or crucifix, placed on it). By passing through the rood screen, you were taking an important step – from the temporal world into the private world of the sacred.

The canons assembled in the choir to worship at set times throughout the day. For daytime services, they would have entered from the cloister, through the door at the east end of the nave. At night, they filed down a stair from the dormitory in the east range. The canons sat in wooden stalls placed along the side walls. Their attention was focused on the presbytery, the raised area at the east end, where the high altar lay. This was the most sacred part of the church. The altar itself was richly dressed and behind it was a retable, a painted timber screen with religious scenes set in panels.

**Above:** Artist's impression of a Requiem Mass in the priory church, around 1400.

**Right:** The tall east window lighting the choir and presbytery.

**Opposite right:** The sedilia, used as seats by the priest and his assistants during services.

**Opposite far right:** The piscina and aumbry set into the presbytery's south wall.

The lower parts of some of the presbytery windows were blocked at some time in the priory's history. In the case of the tall east windows, this might have been related to the installation of the retable. In the early 20th century, the blocking was removed and fragments of stained glass were found. The tracery dividing the east windows was decorated with four carved-stone faces, two of which still survive.

Set into the south wall are three features which had important roles in the celebration of the Mass. The three fine seats, or sedilia, were occupied by the priest and his assistants during the service. They are among the earliest sedilia to survive in Scotland. Further along the wall is the piscina, or basin, in which the priest ritually rinsed his hands and washed the sacred vessels during the Mass. The water drained through a stone basin into the ground outside the church, thus ensuring that everything associated with the transformation of the bread and wine into the body and blood of Christ remained on consecrated ground. The aumbry, or small cupboard, was perhaps the Easter sepulchre, where the consecrated Host and crucifix were kept safe until Easter Day.

The door through the north wall led to the sacristy, a lean-to building of which only the lower part of the walls remains. The priestly vestments and sacred vessels used for the Mass were stored here, in securely padlocked and iron-bound chests.

# THE CLOISTER

T he principal domestic buildings of the priory were arranged around a quadrangle. A covered walkway ran along the inner faces of the buildings, with an open space or 'garth' at the centre, which may have had a garden to provide flowers for the altars. The canons used the cloister for quiet prayer, contemplation and reading.

Cloisters were built to a standardised plan derived from the Benedictine monasteries of mainland Europe, which forms the basic layout of most monastic foundations. However, each site has features which make it unique. Most of the buildings surrounding the cloister at Inchmahome date to the 15th century. They replaced earlier buildings on approximately the same site. The buildings were arranged over two floors. They would have been harled (plastered with a coat of lime and sand) to keep them waterproof and covered by pitched slated roofs.

The east range is well preserved. Here you can see the remains of the chapter house, warming house and kitchen, as well as drains for the latrines on the first floor. Part of the day stair also survives. It led up to the canons' dormitory, which ran the length of the upper floor. The chapter house was on the ground floor of the east range. Its pitched roof is a later addition (see pages 14–15).

At the SE corner of the dormitory was the latrine block. The latrines were emptied directly into the drain at ground level.

The first floor of the south range was occupied by the refectory or dining hall. Little remains of the west range. The flight of stairs at the SW corner of the cloister may have led up to the prior's lodgings. This range may also have provided guest accommodation.

**Opposite:** A view of the cloister from the SW.

**Right:** The walkway along the eastern side of the cloister.

# THE CHAPTER HOUSE

The chapter house was the second most important building in the priory, behind the church. Here the business of the priory was discussed and discipline maintained. The canons met here every morning.

Inchmahome's chapter house is a rectangular room, with stone benches set around its sides. The canons would gather here to listen to readings from the martyrology and the Rule of St Augustine from a lectern. Deceased members of the house and benefactors were commemorated before the business of the day was attended to.

**Above:** The chapter house. The pitched roof was added in the 17th century, when the building was converted to a mausoleum.

**Opposite top, left and centre:** Incised grave slabs representing a knight drawing his sword (left) and John Drummond of Menteith (right).

**Opposite top right:** An grave slab with interlace pattern cross-head and sword.

In the 17th century, the building was transformed into a mausoleum. This is thought to have been for Lord Kilpont, son of the 7th Earl of the Graham line, who was murdered in the camp of his kinsman, the Marquis of Montrose, in 1644. Upon the death of the last earl in 1694, the building was extended west to create an avenue. This extension was removed in the 1920s to bring the front of the building back in line with the rest of the east range.

Today the chapter house shelters memorials brought in from the church for their better protection, together with fragments of carved stones which once adorned the priory buildings. The most striking monument is the double effigy of Walter Stewart (died 1295) entwined with his countess, Mary. Theirs is a very unusual pose, a touching departure from the martial and pious poses which are more common in medieval memorials. A second effigy depicts an armed knight with the Stewart arms emblazoned on his shield, possibly Sir John de Menteith who died in the early 14th century. Another 14th-century gravestone depicts Sir John Drummond carrying a spear and shield. The Drummonds were generous benefactors. Sir John's father, Malcolm, endowed the priory with his estate of Cardross near Dumbarton.

# OTHER DOMESTIC BUILDINGS

**W**e cannot be sure how the other buildings in the complex were used. It is certainly possible that the functions of individual rooms were altered during the three centuries of the priory's life.

The large room at the south of the east range has a large double fireplace in its south wall. This may have been the warming house, where the canons were permitted to warm themselves in cold weather. However, the east wall has a sink, a slop basin and a drain, which suggests this area might have served as a kitchen. Its position is unusual and it may be a later addition. The adjacent day stair linked the first-floor dormitory to the cloister walk in the daytime.

The canons ate one meal in winter and at Lent and two in the summer. Meat was forbidden in the refectory, although fowl was sometimes allowed. An allowance known as a pittance was granted on special occasions, permitting some canons to have extra food and wine on Sundays and feast days.

The west range probably provided accommodation for some of the more senior members of the community, such as the cellarer, who was responsible for provisioning the priory. He probably had rooms on the first floor, near those of the prior, with vaulted storage cellars on the ground floor.

**Left:** The southernmost room of the east range, thought to have been a warming house, though its function may have changed during the priory's history.

**Right:** An artist's impression of the dormitory which once occupied the first floor of the east range. The canons are shown making their way down the day stair to the chapter house.

The priory complex would also
have included an infirmary, where
sick and elderly canons were cared
for. The discovery in the 1930s of
some 30 human skulls to the east
of the cloister suggests that the
infirmary and cemetery
may well lie there.

# THE ISLAND AND THE LAKE

T he priory was built in peaceful surroundings of great natural beauty, and it is worth taking a short walk around the island to admire the scenery and wildlife.

Find the path leading west from the pier. It is possible from here to see the neighbouring island of Inch Talla. Depending on the season, the ruined castle of the earls of Menteith may be visible on the island.

The lake was formed at the end of the last ice age, in a depression left by retreating ice. Its water harbours many submerged and emergent plants. It is also rich in invertebrates, including dragonflies, water beetles, stoneflies and mayflies. The vegetation and insects support fish and reptiles which ultimately become the prey of species such as otter and osprey, which can be seen hunting here.

**Left:** The sweet chestnuts on Nun's Walk, thought to date back to the 1500s.

**Top right:** Osprey, which prey on fish and small mammals, can often be seen circling above the lake.

Further along the path, look out for the ancient hazel stools with their tall spindly wands. Hazel, willow and alder would have been managed by coppicing – that is, frequent cutting back to produce long, straight poles. These would have been very useful to the canons – for fencing, tools, handles and in wattle and daub for buildings. Hazel had many uses in medieval times. Its nuts contain as much protein as eggs, seven times as much fat and five times as much carbohydrate. Bundles of branches, called faggots, were used to fuel ovens. The foliage was used as animal fodder.

A short distance inland is Queen Mary's Bower – a little enclosure of trained boxwood trees – and beyond it the sheltered lawn called Queen Mary's Garden. There are also many oaks on the island. These large trees were not coppiced but allowed to grow to supply structural timber. The canons may have allowed pigs to graze on the acorns, but this would have been strictly controlled.

At the south of the island is a small hillock known as Nun's Hill. Legend has it that a nun was buried here in an upright position, having sinned carnally with the earl's son. An avenue called Nun's Walk leads back to the priory, passing on its way three wonderfully twisted sweet chestnut trees. They are believed to have been planted here in the 16th century. The sweet chestnut was probably introduced to Scotland by the Romans, who valued its nuts as food. Unfortunately, this far north the nuts are too small to eat. The tree does not readily establish itself in the wild; it generally needs to be planted. Like oaks, sweet chestnuts have long lives.

The chestnuts at Inchmahome are obviously in poor condition. Their ideal growing conditions are in deep, well-drained soils. The island's soils probably constrain root growth due to the high water table. As the tree ages, the bark splits at an angle, giving the twisted look that lends these trees their character.

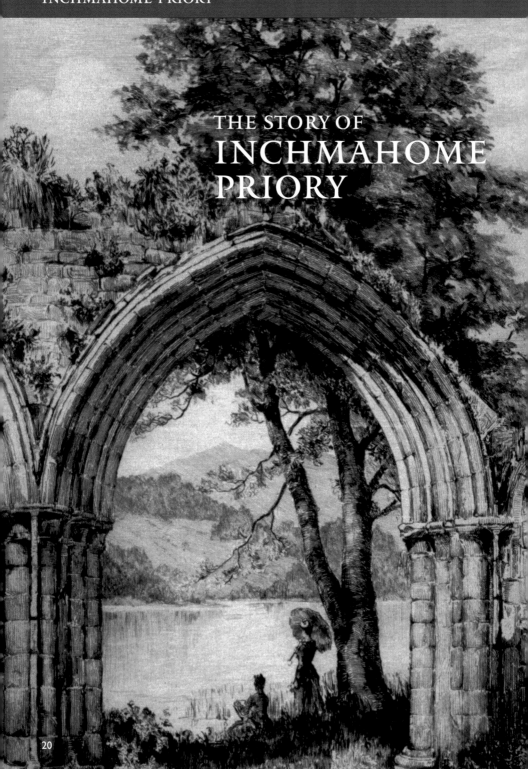

# THE STORY OF
# INCHMAHOME
# PRIORY

Inchmahome Priory was founded by Walter Comyn, in his day one of the most powerful lords in Scotland. From his seat on the neighbouring island of Inch Talla, he invited the canons to the Lake of Mentieth.

Walter Comyn, the founder of Inchmahome, was the second son of William, Earl of Buchan. By the time of his 40th birthday (around 1230), he controlled the vast territory of Badenoch in the central Highlands. In 1233, he married Isabella, Countess of Menteith, and gained control of the lucrative Earldom of Menteith.

Inch Talla, the small island next to Inchmahome, became one of his principal residences. This may have influenced his decision to found a priory on the neighbouring island. Founding a religious community was a pious act. It also provided a kind of 'spiritual insurance', as the residents were bound to pray for the souls of the founder and his family and so speed their passage to Heaven. It was also a declaration of status. The foundation of Inchmahome was Walter's way of announcing that his family had arrived.

Permission for Walter Comyn to found a priory on Inchmahome was granted by the Bishop of Dunblane, following a lengthy dispute between the two over rights to revenue from the churches of Menteith. The foundation was authorised by Pope Gregory IX on 1 July 1238.

'We have ordained that it shall be lawful for the said earl [Walter Comyn, Earl of Menteith] and his successors to build a house for religious men of the order of St. Augustine, in the island of INCHMAQUHOMOK, without impediment or opposition from said bishop [of Dunblane] or his successors'

William, Bishop of Glasgow and Geoffrey, Bishop of Dunkeld, 1238

**Opposite:** A romantic view of Inchmahome by Edward Slocombe, around 1870, shows young ladies enjoying the view across the lake.

**Above:** The coat of arms of the Comyn earls of Buchan.

# THE CANONS ARRIVE

As was often the case with Augustinian foundations, the priory was founded on the site of a pre-existing church. However, the establishment of the priory had implications for all the neighbouring churches. Their revenues were required to support the canons, who in turn had a spiritual duty to minister to their congregations.

Inchmahome Priory was not the first Christian establishment on the island. A passing reference in 1210 to the parson on 'insula Macholem' ('isle of my dear St Colman') appears in the cartulary (records) of Cambuskenneth Abbey. The church on the island was being used as a parish church when the canons arrived.

The foundation of the priory had been granted following the settlement of a dispute over rights to the churches in Menteith between Walter Comyn and the Bishop of Dunblane. The canons were given the right to the revenues of the churches of Leny, Kilmadock and Port, along with at least four chapels. These were located around the edges of the loch, one to the east, one to the west at Arnchly, the third at Chapellaroch to the SW and the fourth on property belonging to the Drummond family.

The Kirk of Port was on the site of the present parish church in Port of Menteith. This became the parish church of the people living around the loch sometime before the end of the 15th century, suggesting that the former parish church on the island was by then the preserve of the canons and their patrons.

The 'Isle of Rest', as it was also known, was well suited to the needs of the canons. It offered them isolation and the potential for self-sufficiency, within a reasonable distance of their mother house at Cambuskenneth and the royal castle at Stirling.

There is no surviving cartulary for Inchmahome. Some original charters have been preserved in the archives of other monasteries. The names of many of the priors survive. Adam is the first prior whose name is known. He appears on the Ragman Roll, the register of Scots forced to swear allegiance to Edward I of England at Berwick in 1296, the beginning of the Wars of Independence.

**Opposite:** The eastern tip of the island, where the jetty once stood.

# THE EARLDOM OF MENTEITH

T he extensive earldom of Menteith was held in the mid–
1200s by the Comyns, one of the most powerful families
in 13th-century Scotland. A power vacuum created by
the death of Inchmahome's founder brought the vast resources
of the earldom into the hands of the House of Stewart.

Menteith was one of the great provinces of medieval Scotland, although
little is known of its earls before 1200. Walter Comyn, who acquired the
earldom in 1233 and established Inchmahome Priory, was the first to
enjoy a significant reputation. His family had enjoyed royal favour since
the reign of Malcolm Canmore (1058–93). Walter was a second son,
and so did not inherit the family's ancestral lands, but this does not
seem have hindered his ascent.

**Left:** The double effigy
of Earl Walter Stewart
and his countess Mary.

**Top:** Earl Walter's coat
of arms.

**Right:** The coat of arms
of Robert Stewart,
Earl of Menteith and
later Duke of Albany.

Walter's sudden death in 1258 led to a struggle for power. His widow Isabella was implicated in his demise, with accusations of poisoning in the air. Walter's nephew John wrested the estate from Isabella and her new English husband Sir John Russell. In 1285 the Comyn lands were split between two heirs. One was William, Walter Comyn's great nephew. The other was Walter Stewart, the husband of Isabella's younger sister Mary, Countess of Menteith.

Walter Stewart, who became Earl of Menteith, was an influential figure in royal and political circles. He distinguished himself at the Battle of Largs in 1263 when Hakon IV of Norway invaded the west of Scotland. He also accompanied Princess Margaret, daughter of Alexander III, to Norway in 1282 for her marriage to Eric II. Walter and his wife Mary were buried in the choir of the priory church at Inchmahome. Their charming double effigy is now on display in the chapter house.

The 'Comyn century' was brought to an end in 1306 with the murder of John Comyn by King Robert I (the Bruce). Bruce visited the priory that year and on two other occasions.

In 1361 Robert Stewart, younger son of Robert II, became the new earl through marriage to Margaret Graham, heiress to the earldom of Menteith. He was later created Duke of Albany and built the mighty castle at Doune. On his son's execution in 1425 most of the Menteith lands reverted to the Crown. They were returned to the Grahams in the late 17th century and have remained in their family ever since.

**Right:** Doune Castle, built by Robert Stewart, Duke of Albany, about ten miles east of Inchmahome.

# THE AUGUSTINIANS

The Rule of St Augustine is the oldest western monastic rule. A set of instructions for the devout life, it was formulated from selected writing by St Augustine, Bishop of Hippo (d. 430).

No one knows whether St Augustine actually wrote the rule, but it inspired thousands of religious communities across Europe. At its heart was the belief that an individual should live a communal, spiritual life, free from worldly temptation.

The Rule of St Augustine was overtaken in the 6th century by the Rule of St Benedict as the most popular monastic precept. However, it came to prominence again in the 11th century in response to a need to improve the discipline of the clergy. The Augustinian canons are also known as 'canons regular' (living to a rule). They were also called the 'Black Canons' after the colour of their habit.

**Right:** Augustinian houses in Scotland:

**1** Holyrood Abbey in Edinburgh

**2** Cambuskenneth Abbey near Stirling

**3** Inchcolm Abbey in the Firth of Forth

**4** Jedburgh Abbey

**Bottom left:** St Augustine depicted on a 15th-century panel.

**Bottom right:** St Dunstan writing out the Rule of St Benedict.

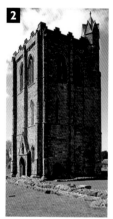

The lives of Benedictine monks and Augustinian canons had many similarities. Both observed the canonical hours and rang the church bells at the start of services. There were subtle differences in how they worshipped, but the greatest distinction was that unlike monks, canons did not live an enclosed life. They were priests with a duty to minister to populations living near their houses. However, as time went by, some communities of canons gave up their pastoral duties in favour of a more monkish existence, blurring the boundaries further.

The Augustinians were one of the most popular choices among founders of religious houses in Britain. In all, 18 Augustinian houses were established in Scotland in the 12th, 13th and 14th centuries, the earliest being Scone Abbey in 1120. In addition to the rule, each house adopted a set of canonical guidelines. This meant they were quite flexible and able to adapt to a range of situations in comparison to the Cistercians or the Benedictines. Augustinian houses were often established on sites which already had a church and would continue to minister to the local population. The Augustinians were also noted for their clerical and managerial skills and for this reason their priories were often located near royal castles and other centres of power.

# LIFE AT THE PRIORY

There were between 10 and 15 canons, including the prior, living on Inchmahome at any one time. Their primary function was *opus dei*, the work of God, which they achieved through worship and prayer.

The monastic day was divided into 12 equal periods, or hours. These were punctuated by the church bells, which marked out seven or eight services spread through the day and night. The bells would have been audible far beyond the church and would have helped ordinary people to structure their day. There were also communal and private Masses to be celebrated each day. In addition to attending services, the canons read and studied. Only a small portion of the day was given over to manual labour such as tending the orchards, gardening or fishing. Augustinian canons were excused from attending the priory church when engaged in their pastoral duties.

The canons spent most of their day in silence. They could only speak in prayer, in praise, to give certain instructions and when in the parlour. At other times, the canons may have used sign language to communicate.

**Left:** Augustinian canons share a silent meal, while listening to a devotional reading.

**Top right:** Choral singing during a church service.

**Right:** Canons washing before a meal.

The different areas of monastic administration were presided over by officers working under instruction from the prior and sub-prior. Although all decisions taken by the community were corporate, the prior was ultimately responsible for the conduct of the priory. Other officers included the master of novices (responsible for instructing new monastic recruits), the chamberlain (in charge of clothing) and the sacrist (who maintained the church furnishings and priestly vestments).

Each canon would receive an allowance for food, drink and material needs. This included a habit siller (clothes allowance), a pittance (small bonus) and a yard or garden. Therefore, the number of canons supported by the priory was dependent on the size of its income.

We know little about the sources and amounts of income which the priory received. However, in 1561, after the Reformation, its minimum annual income was £1,680. By comparison, the Augustinian monasteries at Scone and Holyrood commanded incomes of over £5,000, while St Andrews Cathedral received more than double that.

A charter of 1604 lists the assets of Inchmahome, Dryburgh and Cambuskenneth as 'lands, baronies, castles, towers, patronages, manor-places, mills, multures, salmon and other fishings, woods, parks, meadows, forests, teinds, teindsheaves, annual rents etc'. This picture of a small community with great wealth probably explains an attempt made in 1508 to allocate Inchmahome's revenues to the newly built and expensive Chapel Royal at Stirling.

# A ROYAL VISITOR

**M**ary Queen of Scots' brief stay on the island as a child adds a romantic tinge to the story of Inchmahome, though she was only four years old at the time.

In 1547 the Scots were defeated by the English at the Battle of Pinkie, near Edinburgh. The panic that ensued saw the hurried departure from Stirling to Inchmahome of the dowager Queen Marie de Guise with her daughter, the four-year-old Mary Queen of Scots. The priory was a natural choice. It offered sanctuary close to Stirling, and was under the control of the son of Lord Erskine, little Mary's guardian.

The young queen stayed on the island for just three weeks, but stories abound of her accomplishments. Her name is still attached to the little bower in the centre of the island.

The island's romantic association with Mary reached fever pitch in the 19th century. William Frazer, describing the considerable size of the boxwood trees in the bower, wrote that, 'The desire of tourists to become possessed of the relics of Queen Mary has gradually led to the complete disappearance of nearly the whole of these trees.' New boxwood saplings were planted in 1859.

**Above:** Mary Queen of Scots as a young woman. Her visit to Inchmahome took place in 1547, less than a year before she left Scotland for France.

**Right:** Queen Mary's Bower, the boxwood enclosure SW of the cloister.

# THE CANONS DEPART

E ven before the Protestant Reformation of 1560, the Church in Scotland was undergoing change. Inchmahome Priory was among the monastic houses affected.

During the later Middle Ages, there was a growing tendency to appoint commendators as heads of monasteries. These were royal appointments, not members of the religious order. In Inchmahome's case, the priory was granted to Robert, Master of Erskine in 1529. In 1604, James VI formally granted it to the Erskine family in perpetuity. By then the last canon had been laid to rest.

In the 1600s, the Graham family acquired Inch Talla and Inchmahome, where they created gardens and planted trees. They also transformed the chapter house into a large mausoleum, adding to it a 40m-long avenue terminating in an elaborate gateway. After the priory passed into State care in 1926, the gateway and avenue were removed and the chapter house restored to something approaching its original form.

**Above:**
John Erskine,
Earl of Mar,
one of
Inchmahome's lay
commendators.

### R.B. CUNNINGHAME GRAHAM
Author and adventurer Robert Bontine Cunninghame Graham (1852–1936) is buried in the choir at Inchmahome Priory. The son of a Scottish army officer and a Spanish noblewoman, he travelled the world, making his fortune as a cattle rancher in Argentina, where he was known as Don Roberto. On his travels he befriended Buffalo Bill, Oscar Wilde and the novelist Joseph Conrad. Having served as a Liberal MP, he was instrumental in founding both the Scottish Labour Party and the Scottish National Party. His many achievements include writing books on history, politics and travel, as well as numerous short stories and essays. A man of strong and often radical opinions, he was the first MP ever to be suspended from the House of Commons for swearing.

There are a number of Historic Scotland properties in and around Stirling, a selection of which is shown below.

### STIRLING CASTLE
Medieval stronghold, political power base and pleasure palace of the royal Stewarts: one of Scotland's most spectacular castles.

### CASTLE CAMPBELL AND GARDENS
The elegant Lowland seat of the Campbells stands in a commanding position at the top of spectacular Dollar Glen.

### DOUNE CASTLE
A magnificent castle of the late 14th century, built for Regent Albany and famously used as a location by Monty Python.

### DUNBLANE CATHEDRAL
Built on an ancient Christian site, the medieval cathedral retains its Gothic exterior and red sandstone tower despite restoration.

| | STIRLING CASTLE | CASTLE CAMPBELL | DOUNE CASTLE | DUNBLANE CATHEDRAL |
|---|---|---|---|---|
| ↗ | At the top of Stirling town centre, off the M9 | Ten miles east of Stirling on the A91 | In Doune, 10 miles NW of Stirling on the A84 | In Dunblane, just off the B8033 |
| 🕐 | Open all year | Open all year Winter: closed Thu/Fri | Open all year Winter: closed Thu/Fri | Open all year; closed Sunday mornings |
| 📞 | 01786 450 000 | 01259 742 408 | 01786 841 742 | 01786 823 388 |
| 🚗 | Approx 15 miles from Inchmahome Priory. | Approx 25 miles from Inchmahome Priory. | Approx 10 miles from Inchmahome Priory. | Approx 12 miles from Inchmahome Priory. |

For more information on all Historic Scotland sites, visit **www.historic-scotland.gov.uk**
To order tickets and a wide range of gifts, visit **www.historic-scotland.gov.uk/shop**

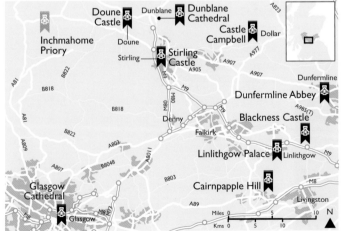

### Key to facilities

| | |
|---|---|
| Car parking | P |
| Bus/coach parking | P |
| Interpretive display | |
| Visitor centre | |
| Reasonable wheelchair access | |
| Shop | |
| Toilets | |
| Disabled toilets | |
| Cafe | |
| Picnic area | |
| Strong footwear recommended | |